The Play
of
Everyman

—

Based on the old English morality play
New Version by Hugo von Hofmannsthal
Set to blank verse by George Sterling
In collaboration with Richard Ordynski

A. M. Robertson
San Francisco
1917

A. M. Robertson
San Francisco,
1917

Wahr
8152
German
1-16-1923

PREFACE

It is to Mr. Richard Ordynski that I am indebted for the privilege and pleasure of setting to English blank verse Hugo von Hofmannsthal's version of "that play of all time," "Everyman."

"Everyman" in the original is a stiff and raw fabric, but destined, perhaps, to outlast many a more gorgeous woof. However, one needs but to read it in its English form to realize the extent to which von Hofmansthal has vivified and humanized the play, adding thereto powerfully of the dramatic and emotional elements. The appeal of "Everyman" to the medieval mind must have been vast, for it was a child's mind, and therefore one to be moved far more greatly by things seen than by things preached. But though the moral pill was deftly enough sugar-coated for the audience of those distant days, "Everyman" can but seem a somewhat crude and unconvincing affair to the pampered and sophisticated public of today. I may perhaps compare it to the stark simplicity of a board-walk, though it has, for that matter, all the directness of such a structure, what of its deadly sincerity. But when, over fifteen years ago, I saw the leading character presented by an actress of charm and talent, it required all of that lady's skill to hold me and my friends.

Von Hofmannsthal has obviated such a need, and his version affords an agreeable and interesting contrast to the bleak and not always intelligible passages of the elder drama. He has, as it were, curved and widened the walk, given it vistas and a decent amount of greenery, and all this without losing sight of his goal—a goal needed no less by the man of today than by the knight, man-at-arms or peasant of old years.

He followed the plan of the English "Everyman," with its rhymed lines, but I have thought it better to make use of blank verse, the breakable lines of which lend an articulation, flexibility and suspense not readily accessible to one who would use the other (and monotonous) form. Moreover, following Mr. Ordynski's valuable suggestions, I have somewhat amplified the play by the addition of the characters of War and a Workman, as well as by the lines in which the Paramour takes her leave of Everyman and those in which the Debtor and the Workman assist Good Deeds. The scene of the Paramour's departure is of especial value, I think, in the appeal and coherence of the play.

GEORGE STERLING.

Los Angeles, Dec. 29th, 1916.

Everyman

Everyman

—

CHARACTERS

—

This version presented for the first time, on
January 9th at the Trinity Auditorium
Los Angeles, California, by

Richard Ordynski and Aline Barnsdall

with the following cast.

CHARACTERS

The Prologue	Marjorie Day
The Voice of God	
Death	Clyde McCoy
The Devil	Percival Vivian
Faith	Veda McEvers
Good Deeds	Violette Wilson
War	Harold Skinner
Mammon	James H. Finlayson
Everyman	Gareth Hughes
Everyman's Mother	Kirah Markham
Friend	Irving Pichel
Paramour	Ann Andrews
The Little Cousin	Margaret T. Allen
The Fat Cousin	Athol Hayes
The Steward	Bruno Schuman
The Cook	Miriam Meredith
A Monk	Gordon Thomas
The Poor Neighbor	George Warren
The Debtor	Ford Tarpley
The Debtor's Wife	Irene Bevans
Workman	Phillip Gastrock
A Servant	George Hackathorn
Guests	The Misses Vernon, Boike, Burgner Collier, Davis, Holmes, Ingham, Moore, Rottman. Messrs. McCullough, Nieto, Sleeper, Vickers.
Servants	Miss LeClerq, Miss Lee, Mr. Williams
Officers	Mr. Curran, Mr. James
Pages	Miss Riley, Miss Dunaway
Musicians	Miss Margrage, Miss Barnes
Angels	Miss Goodall, Miss Hopkins, Miss Michaels, Miss Price

Everyman

PROLOGUE

Listen, good people, to this holy play;
'Tis a performance for the rich and poor,
The small, the great, the children and the old;
And you shall learn that earthly days and deeds
Are frail as they are fleeting. You shall see
When and through whom the final summons came
To one, like you, a mortal. So take heed
And treasure in your hearts the lesson here,
Which we, in all simplicity, will show.
Secure you sit to-day, who shall one day
Go forth on that same road as EVERYMAN.

THE LORD GOD

O men! vile men! how long shall I endure
The hardness of your hearts? Forgetting Me,
Dreading Me not, ye live the lives of beasts,
Basely sin-soaked, blind to My light and law,
And know Me not—your God. The world alone
Enthralls you. Heavenly things beget your scorn.
The bond between My majesty and you
Ye have forgotten—that I gave My blood,
Dying upon the Tree that men might live,—
That I was nailed upon a martyr's cross,—
That cruel thorns were woven for my crown,—
That I gave all to you. Now all my laws
Ye break. But swiftly shall my judgment come
On sinful man. Unerring messenger!

Stand forth!   I have a journey for thee, Death.

DEATH:

Almighty God, behold thy servant! Say
What duty waits, that I may serve Thy will.

THE LORD GOD

Go thou to Everyman and say that he
Must make a pilgrimage upon this day
And hour—a journey he shall not escape.
See that he brings his book of reckoning,
And that he neither tarries nor escapes.

DEATH

Lord, I will roam this whole great earth of Thine,
Relentlessly, and seek out small and great—
All men that cherish Thy commandments not,
But lower than the beasts have sunk.   All hearts
Given to earthly joys my spear shall pierce,
And blinded, they shall find not Heaven's gate.
Ill shall it be with him on that dread day,
Whom Faith and Charity do not befriend!

EVERYMAN:

(*Steps forth from his house, a Servant following.*)
Haste to my steward.   I have word for him.
          (*The Servant returns to the house.*)
How pleasant is my home to look upon!
How costly and how prominent!   Show me
Another one as rich in all the land!
What wealth of furnishings in many rooms!
What coffers and what retinue of serfs!

Money besides is mine, and country seats,
And fertile farms that bring me goodly rents.
My factories, aroar with all their wheels,
Bellow at dawn to summon to their tasks
Unnumbered men. And deep in many mines
My toilers sweat, far from the wholesome day.
Oh, be my future happy as my past!

(*Enter STEWARD.*)

Steward, go bring a well-filled bag of gold,
For I forgot it. Mark you this besides:
A splendid feast I order for to-day:
Kindred and guests are coming. Send the cook,
And bring the gold yourself.
        (*Steward goes within. Cook enters at once.*)
                                Cook, I command
A sumptuous feast to-day.

COOK:

                    Must every course,
Then, be prepared afresh?

EVERYMAN:

                    Plague take you, yes!
Nothing warmed-over for a board like mine!

COOK:

From yesterday at least enough remains
For two cold courses.

EVERYMAN:

                    Dolt! Impertinent!

Shall I eat beggars' food?
(*Cook goes within. Steward appears. Gives bag to
Everyman.*)
        See that you keep
Strict watch on all the servants, man and maid.
They please me not at all.
(*The POOR NEIGHBOR appears, approaching anx-
iously. EVERYMAN'S FRIEND also approaches,
with quick steps.*)
        It is for that
I've set you o'er the rest. But go! here comes
My friend.
      (*Exit Steward.*)
      You've made me wait too long. But now
We'll go and see that property beyond
The city gates. I think it could be made
A pleasure-garden.

FRIEND:
      Order and 'tis done!
He who can pay, needs only say!

POOR NEIGHBOR:
        Kind sir,
Is this the house of wealthy Everyman?
O sir! I beg you in my poverty!
Give alms to a poor man!

FRIEND:
    (*To Everyman.*)
      Now, as I said,
We must make haste: we cannot linger long.

POOR NEIGHBOR:

(*Stretches his hands beseechingly.*)
O Everyman! have pity!

FRIEND:

Do you not
Recall his face?

EVERYMAN:

I? Who is he?

POOR NEIGHBOR:

I stretch
My hands to you, O Everyman! for I
Knew better days, and was your neighbor once,
Before they took my home away from me.

EVERYMAN:

(*Giving him a coin.*)
Enough!

POOR NEIGHBOR:

(*Does not take coin.*)
A stingy offering!

EVERYMAN:

Say you so?
Odds truth!

POOR NEIGHBOR:

Had I a brother's share therefrom,
I should be well and happy.

EVERYMAN:

You? Therefrom?

POOR NEIGHBOR:

Because of this, O Everyman! I kneel
Before you. Do but share that bag with me!

EVERYMAN:

(*Laughs*)

Merely that?

FRIEND:

What a man has, he keeps a grip upon;
You'd have a thousand beggars round your neck,
Elsewise. A hundred thousand!

POOR NEIGHBOR:

But you are
So rich! Why, if you gave me half the purse,
You'd still have all the coffers in your house,
And rents and interest.

EVERYMAN:

Man, who are you
That you should prate of coffers and of rents
Or of my income?

FRIEND:

I should be ashamed!

EVERYMAN:

Quit, man! For you are greatly in the wrong,

If still you dream that I could please myself
In sharing this with you. 'Tis mine no more,
But must be paid to-day as purchase-price
Upon a pleasure-garden. So 'tis pledged,
And he who sells the garden will not wait.

POOR NEIGHBOR:

Well, pay him every penny. You have but
To say a word and they will bring you more;
For if you have one purse, you must have ten.
Send quickly for another now, and share
This purse with me, if you're a Christian man!

EVERYMAN:

And were another brought, 'twould not be free.
In this hard battle against death and sin,
Still must my money toil for me, must still
Go far afield, and send back interest,
That all my dues be mine indeed. Behold!
My houses cost me greatly, what of horse
And hound and servants and a thousand things
That are in keeping with my state; for I
Have pleasure-gardens, fish ponds, game-preserves,
That need more looking-after than a child.
One must improve estates, and where so much
Goes out, the more there must be to come back.
Oh! easily 'tis said, "That man is rich."
But have you thought what cares we rich men have?
From far and near come flowing claims and needs,
So that one cannot cross the street but what
One meets an outstretched hand. Well, even that
One must expect, but still, no pampering!

Things must be done just so, for there are rules,
Let poor as well as rich observe. To each
His own: this law the beggar violates.
For look you: were I to divide my wealth
Among the needy, there would be for each
I swear, this single shilling, this one coin!
Take then your own just portion, man, and go!
(*Neighbor takes shilling and goes.*)

FRIEND:

You gave him what was just. Money, God knows,
Makes brains!

EVERYMAN:

Come, let us hasten, for the day grows old.
(*Enter DEBTOR, led by TWO OFFICERS, and followed by WIFE and CHILDREN, in rags.*)

FRIEND:

What mother's son is this they hale along,
Arms crossed? A debtors' prison is his goal,
No doubt. Uncareful one! Now he'll have time
On bread and water to consider things,
Or hang his wretched carcass on a nail.
You tried to make a rhyming game of life:
Lending and spending rhyme too well, you see!

DEBTOR:

One must have care with life's broad ledger, else
The account goes wrong.

EVERYMAN:

Now whom have you in mind?

DEBTOR:

The one who asks.

EVERYMAN:

I do not even know
Whom you may take me for.

DEBTOR:

Shame would be mine,
If I were in your shoes!

EVERYMAN:

You give hard words
Without good cause. If life's awry with you,
Am I to blame?

DEBTOR:

What flinty words are these,
For mine that are so soft!

EVERYMAN:

Who deals you them?

DEBTOR:

You, in an evil hour!

EVERYMAN:

I know you not,
Even by sight!

DEBTOR:

Nevertheless your heel
Is on my neck.

EVERYMAN:

That were a strange event,
And I unwitting of it!

DEBTOR:

Yet your name
Brings me to jail.

EVERYMAN:

Now by my patron Saint,
How can this be?

DEBTOR:

You are that Everyman
At whose complaint the law lays hold on me;
I were not dragged to prison save for you.

EVERYMAN:

(*Becoming reserved*)
I, innocent, wash now my hands of this.

DEBTOR:

These serviceable tools believe that they
Harry my flesh and soul, but it is you
Whose will they work. You bring this shame on you,
And should feel humbled to the very ground.

EVERYMAN:

Why, in the first place, got you into debt?
You reap but what you sow. My money has
No eyes. It works without regard to you
Or even me. Your only just complaint

Is that you were unready when the debt
Fell due.

DEBTOR:

   He jeers and mocks at my despair.
So, that is to be rich! The heart of such
Knows naught of God's commands. His coffers hold
The pledges of the poor, yet does he keep
The poor in neediness and misery!

DEBTOR'S WIFE:

Be merciful! Tear up the accursed pledge,
Nor send my children's father to a jail!
They never did you harm. Have you, alas!
No honor and no conscience? Can you, then,
List to the orphan's curse unmoved? Do you
Think not on that more dreadful Book of Debts
That opens when life ends?

EVERYMAN:

     Woman, you prate
Of things beyond your understanding. This
I do not out of malice; care and thought
Were given ere we ordered this complaint.
Why, money is the same as other goods,
And has an equal right before the law.

FRIEND:

Ill were it with the world were things not so!

DEBTOR'S WIFE:

But money is mere metal that we grant

In mercy as a loan to fellow-men.

DEBTOR:

Money is not at all as other goods.
'Tis curst and magical, and he whose hand
Reaches for it shall close upon disgrace
And harm immedicable to his soul.
The name of Satan's net in this sad world
Is money.

EVERYMAN:

   What a slanderous fool you are!
You do not know my use to fellow-men.
You feign a scorn of money, yet it is
A godly thing to you. You say 'tis naught;
But you are like the fox that cried, "Sour grapes!"
He who belittles what is not his own
Finds no believers in his honesty.

DEBTOR:

This my misfortune grants me—that I see
The devil's trap, and loose my soul from it,
From money's trap.

FRIEND:

   Loosed are you from that trap,
And for that freedom all your freedom lose.

EVERYMAN:

He who invented money was most wise,
Believe me. Money lifts the world above
All mean exchange and barter, and each man

In his own sphere is as a lesser God.
Through money he does much; and quietly,
With small a-do, he rules a hundred lands,
Being regent of them all.   And naught so high
Or swift that money cannot compass it.
It buys the land and all the serfs thereon—
This by the precious and eternal right,
Ordained by Christ, of our great Emperor.
Yea! that, for money, one may ever buy!
Beyond this power I know no other power,
And all men must bow down in reverence
To what I hold before you in this hand.

DEBTOR'S WIFE:

Swift in the devil's praises!   Man, your jaw
Works like a preacher's!   Mammon's filthy purse
You honor as a holy Tabernacle!

EVERYMAN:

Honor where honor's due!   I blaspheme not
The power I feel existant.

FRIEND:

Enough!

DEBTOR:

(As officers take him away)
        My own, my dearest wife,
Of what avail your weeping?   Mammon's claws
Sink in my soul.   Why gave I him my life?
Now life is over.
            (They take him away)

DEBTOR'S WIFE:

Stand you there like stones?
Is't possible? Where shall I shelter now
My children?

EVERYMAN:

(*To Friend*)
For my sake go quietly
And look into this matter. The man goes
To prison: there's no help for that. But I
Will grant the wife a shelter. What she needs
For mere existence—she and her small brood—
I'll give her, through my steward. They shall go
Into seclusion, where I cannot hear
Her wails, nor know the fullness of her need,
For such things are disgusting. So it goes:
One lives on quietly and decently,
With nothing very bad upon one's mind,
Then all at once one finds the devil to pay:
You're in a mess, not even knowing why!
Why should my sweet tranquillity be spoiled
And I dragged into this vile quarrel—mixt
With this gaunt rogue's misfortune? He has made
His bed: now let him lie in it! He cries
"Oh!" and "Alas!" Just so B follows A.
What then did he expect? It has been so
Since Adam's time: it is no modern thing.
On the shoulders of his very creditor
He wants to pile his burden! But I say
Endurance, patience, gave me power to lend.
He took my money swift enough, and now

It wearies me! But twilight's on the land,
And we have still the pleasure-park to see.
Do me a favor, friend, and that at once:
Make the first payment for me, since delay
Means trouble.   I desire this pleasure-park
And house thereon for a sweetheart of mine:
It soon will be her birthday.

FRIEND:

                         Shall I find
Her with you in the evening?   Well, I'll bring
The bill of sale there, duly made to your
Instructions.

EVERYMAN:

                    Many thanks, good friend! They urge
That I come quickly.   'Tis the only place
In all the world where nothing galls my bliss.
The love she brings is perfect happiness:
So would I bind her with this birthday gift,
That each may see the other's gratitude
Revealed as by twin mirrors.

FRIEND:

                              In what way
Will you do this?

EVERYMAN:

I shall make speedily the garden, then
Place midmost there a lordly pleasure-house.
This I shall build after my own design,
Half-open to the airs, with onyx shafts.
Fountains and lovely bronzes shall be there

And dawn and twilight from surrounding lawns
Shall waft the fragrance of unnumbered flow'rs.
Carnation, rose and lily shall abound,
And wall and arch of woven greenery,
Where even by noon's heat shall we find shade—
Hidden from sunlight in that peaceful place.
There too, in closes sheltered from the wind,
And girt with flowers, a statue shall be set,
Gazing forever in a brimming pool
That flows from marble water-cool and smooth—
The rippling bed of crystal for a nymph.

FRIEND:

Be sure that this will be a costly thing,
Nor shall its like be found with ease.

EVERYMAN:

                         I will
Present it to my dearest one, and take
Her hands in mine, and lead her to the spot.
There in that lovely garden shall she see
Her mirrored face, she who delights me so,
Even as such a garden, with its warmth
And gracious shade.
           (*WORKMAN approaches.*)

FRIEND:

                But see that sorry knave!
He spoils the very air! Will you permit
Such creatures in your presence?

WORKMAN

               Everyman!

Great master, Everyman! give ear to me
A little, I beseech you! Heavy toil
Has stolen youth and grace from me, but I
Am still your fellow man.

EVERYMAN:

What would you here?

WORKMAN

Age comes upon me, and my hand grows slow.
My labor is too much for me. From dawn
To dark I slave for you, as I have slaved
Since boyhood. Grant a pittance for mine age,
And rest from labor in a humble cot,
Far from the city's noise and smoke!

EVERYMAN:

Get hence!
Back to your toil! So long as you have strength,
That long shall I have need of all your days.
These laborers! For what, think you, am I
Set over you by justice and the Lord?
Unless there be a master, who shall toil?
Unless you toil, our scheme of life dissolves,
And all's confusion! From your myriad tasks
Spring art and science and all pleasant things—
Wisdom and beauty and all human ease.
God grant I blot no instant of your work!

WORKMAN

Your yoke is very heavy. Know you not
How hard a thing it is to sweat and toil

A whole life through, and find when age has come
An empty larder and a fireless hearth?
We are as buffers between you and pain,
Enduring heat and cold and weariness,
That heat and cold and weariness be not
Your portion. At the banquet-board of life
Gorge not yourselves: we too would eat the bread
Our hands have earned. Be mindful of our need.
We ask so little and we give so much!

EVERYMAN:

Continue then, to give! It well may be
That in the future better things shall come,
And briefer toil be yours. But I am set
Lord of to-day, and see no present need
To abate the labor. Get you to your task!

WORKMAN:

God grant you clearer sight and kinder heart!
(*Exit Workman.*)
(*Lullaby music is heard.*)

EVERYMAN:

What is it that I hear? What simple strains
Are those? The cradle music of old years
Hides me a moment from the moment's care.
I seem a child again and hear once more
Forgotten accents. Holy memories
Bring to my heart a mother's tenderness.
But say, can this be she? I've little time,
Yet really do not like to run away.

EVERYMAN'S MOTHER:

(*Entering.*)

Oh! I rejoice, my dear and only son,
To see you here! My heart has been full sore
To see your own so set on worldly things,
And with so little time for me.

EVERYMAN:

Night air
Is treacherous, dear mother, and your health
So delicate! It troubles me to see
You out-of-doors: is not in-doors the best?

EVERYMAN'S MOTHER:

And will you come and stay with me?

EVERYMAN~~'S MOTHER~~:

To-night
I cannot.

EVERYMAN'S MOTHER:

Do not let it vex you, then,
That I should keep you by the wayside.

EVERYMAN:

Ah!
My only thought is of your health. Perhaps
Another time were better.

EVERYMAN'S MOTHER:

Do not mind
About my health: I've one foot in the grave

I care not for the present, but for my
Salvation everlasting. Nay! frown not,
My son, at this my preachment. Would it, then,
Be burdensome if I should question you
Whether your soul is dedicate to God?
You step back with impatience, and increase
Your sins of conscience, who should rather look
Within, and meekly see your God aright.
Think! if a message came from Him to you,
Ere morning, with the summons that you go
And render the account of all your life
Before the terrors of His judgment-seat!

EVERYMAN:

My mother, I have no intent to jeer,
Though knowing how priests love to threaten us.
'Tis their one earthly aim, to rail against
Our money, that that money may be theirs.
How well they know to grasp it! It is grief,
Recalling how they fill the hoary heads
Of old sick folk with dark and gloomy thoughts.

EVERYMAN'S MOTHER:

Darkness is otherwhere! Such thoughts are light—
Oh! brightest radiance! The righteous man
Has courage from the issues of this life
And pure rejoicing at the hour of death,
Becoming then aware of happiness.
If sons would think of their last hour, the hearts
Of mothers were less burdened down with woe.

EVERYMAN:

We are good Christians, for we go to church,
Give alms, and do our duty.

EVERYMAN'S MOTHER:

How shall it be
When the last trumpet sounds, and you must give
Such strict account as shows your wealth has bought
Eternal death or else eternal life?
My son, it is a grievous thing to die,
But a more grievous thing to die forever.

EVERYMAN:

I still am young, and is it likely then
That I shall say farewell to earthly joys?

EVERYMAN'S MOTHER:

And will you bury in the sand your head,
To hide the sight of Death's approach, my son?
Lo! he may come to-morrow!

EVERYMAN:

I am fresh
In heart and limb, and will enjoy to-day.
Penance and meditation well may wait
A time more fitting.

EVERYMAN'S MOTHER:

Like the shifting sand
Life changes; but the mind is slow to change.

EVERYMAN:

What doleful talk! I have no time to-day,
As I've already told you.

EVERYMAN'S MOTHER:

My dear son!

EVERYMAN:

But otherwise I am obedient,
And at your service.

EVERYMAN'S MOTHER:

Ah! my talk is sad
To you, which makes it doubly hard to me.
I have a dark presentiment, my son,
I shall not trouble you for many days
With admonitions. I shall burden you
But little longer. Soon the last farewell
Must pass between us two. You will remain
Behind, my child who would not heed advice.
And so I say I do not wish to preach—
Be sure of that. But ah! to your Lord God
Be grateful, for his mercy, and the seven
Great holy sacraments. Each is our aid,
And we so weak! So marvellous their help
On the uncertain journey of this life!

EVERYMAN:

What would you that I do?

EVERYMAN'S MOTHER:

My son, you are

A comely man, fit for a woman's love.
Our Saviour knows man's needs, and knows as well
To shape the common things of earth to man's
Salvation. He has made a sacrament
To turn the lust of man to holiness.
Will you, to serve that lust, estrange yourself
From holy matrimony?

EVERYMAN:

         Oh! I've heard
All that before!

EVERYMAN'S MOTHER:

        And is your heart unchanged?

EVERYMAN:

The right time has not come for it.

EVERYMAN'S MOTHER:

          And yet
Death is so near already!

EVERYMAN:

        Well, I don't
Say "no." Nor, for that matter, "yes."

EVERYMAN'S MOTHER:

          So I
Must live my life in fear?

EVERYMAN:

        Well, as to that,
To-morrow is another day.

EVERYMAN'S MOTHER:

                    Who knows
If he will see it?

EVERYMAN:

                    Trouble not yourself;
You'll see me married yet.

EVERYMAN'S MOTHER:

                    My dearest son,
For those words will I bless you evermore!
Ah! how I thank you, and rejoice that such
Fair words are on your lips!

EVERYMAN:

                    Nor do I speak
In idle chatter.

EVERYMAN'S MOTHER:

                    God be praised your will
Is not against this thing! A little word
Can fill a mother's heart with happiness;
And though your good intentions are but weak,
Yet are they good, not evil, and your speech
Has lifted from my mind a heavy load.

EVERYMAN:

Good-night, then, mother mine, and gentle sleep
Be yours!

EVERYMAN'S MOTHER:

    Good-night to you, my darling son!

Your words are as a music in my heart
More beautiful than flutes and tender chime
Of silvern cymbals. In these latter days
Strange sights and signs are with me. These I take
To be a portent of my early death.
                    (*Exit*)

EVERYMAN:

Why, I too hear a music such as that!
Shall I too háve that portent? Nay—I think
The cause is natural, though to me unknown.
Yet now it falls not only on the ear
But on the eye.
(*PARAMOUR comes on, accompanied by players and
            boys carrying torches.*)
                    Oh! 'tis my light o' love!
My heart is hot for her. Musicians too!
This is a merry crowd that comes for me!

PARAMOUR:

The one who makes us wait becomes by that
The worthiest guest. With cymbal and with torch
We'll have to lead him to his duty.

EVERYMAN:

            *   You
Dim all the torches with your own fair light!
Sweeter your voice than any flute! To-night
All this is like soft balsam to a wound.

PARAMOUR:

It seemed to me, before I drew so near,

Another one had grieved you, and your brow
And your bright cheeks were clouded as with pain.

EVERYMAN:

Oh! am I then so dear to you, my Sweet,
That you have eyes for this? I can but feel,
So madly have I lived in my few years,
I should seem old and broken in your sight.

PARAMOUR:

You wound me by such words! I had not thought
You could say that. I hate these callow youths.
You are my lover and my darling one!

EVERYMAN:

At heart I feel as young as any youth,
And, if a boy no longer, all the more
Is my free spirit young and sensitive.

PARAMOUR:

A youth is raw, loves crudely, but a man
Is gentle and great-hearted. So he draws
All women to him by his tenderness
And poise of soul.

EVERYMAN:

           Had one his death in mind,
And, sunk in melancholy, should behold
Your loveliness, he'd pity his own pain.

PARAMOUR:

The very word affrights! Ah! Death is like

A wicked serpent hidden under flow'rs.
Never let it be wakened!

EVERYMAN:

Love, do I
Bring sorrow to you? Let us bury it
In flowers, nor have a serpent in our thoughts.
And yet two serpents sweetly may embrace.

PARAMOUR:

Serpents embrace? And who, then, may they be?

EVERYMAN:

Your two dear arms wherein I long to rest!
(*She kisses him and places on his head a gay wreath that
a boy hands her. Other boys go by strewing flowers
and sweet-scented herbs. A table comes up through
the floor, lighted and richly covered. Everyman and
Paramour go to the staircase that leads upward. The
guests, ten youths and ten maidens, enter from both
sides, dancing and singing.*)

FIRST SINGER:

A friend invites us, Everyman his name.
A right good sort he is, and has as well
A loving sweetheart. Loneliness he hates,
So bids us here, and merrily we come.
Now sing we one and all, my comrades brave!
(*They sing.*)

SONG

A thousand flowers to crown the feast,

And laughter evermore!
Sing till the sun is in the East,
For Love is at the door!

Bring golden wine and ruddy wine
To brim our glasses o'er!
Let joy be yours and joy be mine,
For Love is at the door!

A toast to you, companions dear,
And bliss unknown before!
Farewell to care, farewell to fear,
For Love is at the door!

EVERYMAN:

Welcome to all, for all can show me soon
The last funereal honors!

A MAIDEN:

What a way

To welcome us!

FAT COUSIN:

Confound it, Everyman,
What sort of greeting call you this? Saint Pan!
What ails you?

PARAMOUR:

What's your trouble, dear?

EVERYMAN:

The mood

Came on me for no reason. Heartily
I welcome you!

(A clash of steel is heard and WAR enters.)
Who's here?

WAR:

                          Come now with me
O Everyman! I've other work for you
Than love and feasting.

EVERYMAN:

        Tell me more.

. WAR:

                              The king
Has planned a war and needs you in his ranks.
Come quickly; bid farewell to home and kin!

FAT COUSIN:

Why break our peaceful days?

WAR:

                Peace makes you fat.

THIN COUSIN:

What! Would you mar our dear prosperity,
And we so comfortable?

WAR:

                      All things end!
War follows upon peace as peace on war!

EVERYMAN:

Why is this war?

WAR:

'Tis the king's will. He deems
His honor has been slighted.

EVERYMAN:

Let him then
Himself avenge that honor.

WAR:

Such is not
The use of kings: when one has vexed a throne,
The humble must allay, with blood and tears,
That injury.

EVERYMAN:

What folly! I go not!

WAR:

Stay then! A mightier than I shall come,
And at his summons shall you hasten forth.
(*Exit.*)

PARAMOUR:

Good riddance! Now be seated as you like,
And servants, pass the wine around. Why stand
And stare so strangely?
(*They seat themselves.*)

EVERYMAN:

All are in their shrouds!

PARAMOUR:

What ails you?   Are you ill?

EVERYMAN:

Ah-ha-ha-ha!
A foolish thought!   I'll drink a cup of wine:
It clears the brain of mildew.

PARAMOUR:

Sit you down.
Say a kind word to them.

EVERYMAN:

Folk, can this be
The house you sought?   You all look strange to me.
(*Silence.*)

THIN COUSIN:

Odds Truth, my cousin Everyman, would you
That we go hence again?

FAT COUSIN:

Easier to say
Than do, when you've so good a cook, and when
The blood is warm with wine.   I'm happy here!

EVERYMAN:

Well, only this: it popped into my mind,
As you came in, how I could buy you up,
Each one, and then sell each and all again,
With no more fuss than if I broke an egg.

A GUEST:

Why this rude speech?

A MAIDEN:

What means he?

PARAMOUR:

Is this meant
Also for me?

(*Everyman looks at her.*)

A GUEST:

Truly a rich man's speech,
Insolent, arrogant!

PARAMOUR:

Fearful is your gaze,
And very strange! Why punish me like this?
Oh, speak!

EVERYMAN:

My love, far be it from my thoughts
To punish you! I love you, O desire
Of all my soul! I did but chance to think
How that sweet face would look and how you'd act,
If you were told that I this hour must die.

PARAMOUR:

For Christ's dear sake, what mean you?   Dearest one
And lover true! I am beside you now—
Look on me, who indeed am yours today
As I shall be forever!

EVERYMAN:

Did I, then,
Request that you stay with me evermore,
Be my companion there as here? would you
Go with me to that final place and share
Mine icy bed? It would be pain to me
If this dread question brought you to my feet,
Fainting and senseless. Yet, if still I tempt
Your faltering steps along that awful path,
Would not your blood stand frozen in your veins?
Oh! it would be a double death to me—
The gall and vinegar of martyrdom—
If then with my own eyes I should behold
Your vows meant nothing! If your hands unclasped
From these cold hands, and your false lips withdrew
From mine, refusing me the final kiss—
Alas!

(*He sighs.*)

PARAMOUR:

Dear guests and cousins, my beloved seems
So strange today! I know not what to do:
Give me your counsel.
(*Everyman stares in front of him and removes garland from
his head.*)
See, he sits aloof,
Sadly, and says strange things. Oh! ne'er before
Saw I him so. I know not what befalls.

THIN COUSIN:

Plague take this silly melancholia!
My cousin, 'tis but that, and if 'tis not,

Why, what's amiss?

FAT COUSIN:

I say it's all within—
A dryness of the brain. My sire oft had
The same complaint. Drink bravely, and the wine
Will moisten the dry brain.

A MAIDEN:

Put in his wine
Some magic: hellebore, violets or hemp.

FAT COUSIN:

Here, boys! Make hot the wine, so that it steams!
Put cinnamon and ginger in it, too!
(*At the back they make the wine glow in a pan.*)

ANOTHER MAIDEN:

I've heard folks say there is a magic stone
Found in the swallow's gizzard. It is used
By great physicians. Chelidonius
'Tis called.

THIN COUSIN:

No, Chalcedon. I've heard of it:
A sovran cure for melancholia.

A THIRD MAIDEN:

I think he should be cured by sympathy.
There is some hidden malice here. Were my
Beloved'ill like this I'd surely try
A cure of mine.

SECOND MAIDEN:

What would you try?

THIRD MAIDEN:

It is

A secret that, if known to common folk,
Would lose its charm.

SECOND MAIDEN:

And where got you this lore?

THIRD MAIDEN:

Suffice you that I got it. Not for you
The secret! But I'll whisper in *her* ear.
(*Rises and whispers in Paramour's ear. At the same time,
further down the table, several talk as follows.*)

A GUEST:

All this is from high living. It must be
His blood's too thick. A poor and needy man
Would not have melancholia.

A MAIDEN:

Why do not
Our music-makers drive our sorrow hence
With mirth of trumpet and of violin?

ANOTHER MAIDEN:

Let's sing! The sick are often cured that way.

A GUEST:

But let the song be modest, surely.

ANOTHER GUEST:

                                        She
Sings only gently, and with tenderness.

ANOTHER GUEST:

Know you the song beginning in this wise?
"In sweetest joys, so fly the hours."   Methinks
Should he hear that, he'd not be sick for long.

FIRST MAIDEN:

No! stop! are we, then, priests?   What good is there
In holy songs for us?

GUEST:

                        'Tis not a priest's!
The very watchmen sing it on the walls
At sunrise.

FIRST MAIDEN:

                Well, I know another song
Less like it.

ANOTHER MAIDEN:

                        What?

GUEST:

(*Kissing her.*)
Oh! "When it rains it's wet!"

OTHER MAIDEN:

"The woods are full of greenery,
But for my lover I am sad.

He rode away, my darling lad,
And who in songs shall woo poor me?"

ANOTHER GUEST:

(*Repeats it mockingly.*)
"Are woods so full of greenery?
And where is your beloved gone?"
(*Meanwhile Everyman has drunk the cup of hot wine, and
looks happier.*)

EVERYMAN:

Be gay, my cousins and my cherished guests!
I've not been very well, but this good wine
Has brought me to my senses.   Greeting now,
To one and all!   It was as though my heart
Had turned to very lead, but stronger now
Burns my desire to live.   How glad am I
We're all together!   I could weep for joy,
My heart's so full.   I have no words for it.
This world's so full of things beyond all price,
And glad am I to be amid them.   Yes,
Friendship and love: the two are worth so much!
He who has both needs naught beside.   Add wine
And music's voice, and lo! the cup o'erflows!
I love you well, sweet guests, and pray that you
Enjoy the moment fully, holding close
And tenderly your dear ones.   Ah! make use
Of this fair hour with all your faculties—
With hands and eyes and hearts and kissing mouths!
Let me not need entreat you more, dear guests!
And you, beloved cousin: sing to us!

FAT COUSIN:

Alack! alas! my skinny brother's called!
Now comes the eternal song about "cold snow!"
(They sing with laughter.)

THIN COUSIN:

(Sings.)

"Dear Mrs. Love, hast thou no concern?
I'm in misery: feel me burn!
Cold, cold snow indeed thou art,
To melt with the fire of my choking heart!
Dear Mrs. Love, come along with me,
And all that heart shall be full of glee!"
(All sing. The dull tolling of a bell is heard. Everyman
pushes his glass away.)

EVERYMAN:

What bell is that? It can mean nothing good,
Methinks, so loud and fearsome is the sound!
Now terror strikes my heart! Why tolls that bell,
And at this hour?

A GUEST:

I hear none, far or near.

ANOTHER GUEST:

Has any heard the sound of bells?

A MAIDEN:

Of bells?

Who talks of bells?

ANOTHER GUEST:

    It is not time for Mass.

PARAMOUR:

I pray you, cease not singing!

A GUEST:

        Has a soul

Heard a bell ring?

ANOTHER GUEST:

    (Smiling.)
    Not for my soul it rang!

PARAMOUR:

Let not the song be interrupted, friends!

EVERYMAN:

I prithee, take no heed! Now all is well,
Nor hear I still that tolling.

FAT COUSIN:

        It all comes

From sluggish blood. I'll order swift for you
Some more hot wine.

EVERYMAN:

    Thanks, cousin! Never mind.
*(He seats himself again. Paramour draws nearer to him.
The others sing at the foot of the table: "The woods
are full of greenery," etc. During the singing, Everyman's Friend comes in and seats himself at the table.*

Suddenly many voices are heard, calling.)
VOICES:
Everyman! Everyman! Everyman!
EVERYMAN:
(Jumping up full of fear.)
O God! who calls for me like this? From where
Am I thus called? Ah! never, never more
Shall joy be mine!
FRIEND:
Everyman, I am here!
PARAMOUR:
See, Everyman! here's your dear comrade!
EVERYMAN:
Oh!

Tell me, dear friend, what awful voices cry,
And call for Everyman so terribly?
THIN COUSIN:
Some echo of our singing caught your ear,
EVERYMAN:
Nay! nay! it was cried fearfully and strong,
Not softly! Thus: "Everyman! Everyman!"
More terrible than that: familiar 'twas,
Yet strange, as from the kingdom of the fiends.
And now, because my soul has heard that cry,
I never shall be comforted—ah, nay!
And list! Again! Oh, God! hear you it not?
How terribly they call for Everyman!
(The same call as before is heard.)

PARAMOUR:

I hear no voice.

FAT COUSIN:

Nor I.

THIN COUSIN:

No tiniest echo!

FRIEND:

(Goes nearer to Everyman.)
Your ears deceive you. You are ill indeed.
Should you not now retire?

EVERYMAN:

My strength returns,
Beholding you. I shall not hear that cry
Again. Be seated, friend! Dear guests, feast well,
And be your happiest! Tomorrow I
Will fare to the physician, that this ill
Come back no more.

PARAMOUR:

Yes, sweetheart! Promise that!
For I should die of worriment and fear
To see you thus again.
*(All continue feasting and making love. Everyman rises
anxiously.)*

EVERYMAN:

Now, for God's sake,
My dearest, tell me why the lights grow dim,

And who that is who comes upon me now!
No mortal being paces with such gait!
(*Death appears in the distance. Exeunt most of the guests.*)

DEATH:

Ho! Everyman! And is your heart so glad!
Have you forgotten utterly your God?

EVERYMAN:

What ask you at this hour? What your concern?
Who are you and what will you?

DEATH:

                           I am sent
From your Creator's majesty for you—
Sent in great haste, and therefore am I here!

EVERYMAN:

       (*Clutching at his heart.*)
What! sent for me?
                (*With scorn.*)
            Indeed, a pretty tale!

DEATH:

And as you give Him little reverence,
So He, remembering on His heavenly throne,
Shows like concern for you.

EVERYMAN:

     (*Following him with downcast eyes.*)
             What would my God
Of me?

DEATH:

That do I here announce: He wills
That now you settle your account with Him.

EVERYMAN:

Oh! I am ill-prepared for such account!
Nay! Must it be? Alas! despair is mine!
But you—I know you not: declare to me
Your nature and your title.

DEATH:

I am Death
Each man I summon, and no man I spare.

EVERYMAN:

What! Will you give no respite even to me?
And worse: to catch me merry, and unwarned!
Odds truth! You do not play the game! 'Twill bring
You little honor. Let me tell you now
I'm unprepared. The ledger of my life
Is far from ready. Give me ten years more,
And it shall be in order, that no fear
May worry me, I swear to you on God!
So, out of God's good mercy, let me stay
And put accounts in order!

DEATH:

Neither cries
Nor prayers avail: the journey must be made
And now.

EVERYMAN:

       O God of mercy, on thy throne,
Have pity on my dire distress! O Death,
Shall I have no companion, none but you,
Upon this journey? Must I leave this earth
Without a comrade—I, who never yet
Have been without companions here below?

DEATH:

Companionship ends now. Wring not your hands:
'Tis useless. Hasten! Go before God's throne
And know your just deserts. Poor fool! to dream
That life and wealth were utterly your own!

EVERYMAN:

Indeed I thought so truly.

DEATH:

               Nay, not so!
Your wealth was but a loan, which now, you gone,
Another shall inherit; and full soon
That other's hour shall strike, and he in turn
Shall bid farewell to all and wander forth.
Yea! I come quickly!

EVERYMAN:

             Just a day! This night!
This hour ere sunrise, that, in penitence
I may hear holy words and be prepared
The better to go with you!

DEATH:

Who are you
To ask delay of Death? Say when I spared
A victim? When I find the one I seek,
Without a warning swiftly at his heart
I strike.

EVERYMAN:

Now must I weep!   Alas!

DEATH:

To weep
Is loss of time.

EVERYMAN:

Woe's me!   How now shall I
Begin? Ah! had I but a little hour—
A single hour to find a comrade in!
To think that I, a mother's child, must go
Alone before my Judge!

DEATH:

Oh! dream you then
That such a one exists? There is no man
But would refuse such service!

EVERYMAN:

Not alone
Before the Judge! Ah! grant a little time,
For speech and counsel!   For the sake of Christ!
For God's dear mercy!

DEATH:

Greatly care not I,
And leave you for a space. But mark! Waste not
A second's time, but use it carefully,
As best becomes a Christian.
(Becomes invisible.)

EVERYMAN:

(Approaching his friend.)
Dearest friend,
You know—

FRIEND:

I know indeed, good Everyman,
And was scarce ten feet distant when Death came.
I heard all things you talked of, and my heart
Was in my throat. A merry man you were—
Sound to the core until this fatal day;
But gazing on you now, oh! I could weep!

EVERYMAN:

Accept my thanks, good friend.

FRIEND:

How may I be
Of aid? Tell me at once!

EVERYMAN:

Truly you are
A faithful friend: I've always found you so.

FRIEND:

So shall you ever find me! Be assured

That were your journey all the way to Hell,
Here will you find a fellow-traveler,
Ready to go with you.

EVERYMAN:

Now may God grant
That I prove worthy of a friend like this!

FRIEND:

Speak not of being worthy! It were shame
If words alone were mine, not deeds.

EVERYMAN:

My friend!

FRIEND:

Speak freely then. Speak frankly. I will stand
As your true comrade in the final hour.
(*Everyman is about to open his mouth.*)
Sorely your sorrow hurts me. May all cares
Of earth decay! Has someone injured you?
Then must you be avenged, and by this hand,
Grasping the blade! Yea! though I die for it!

EVERYMAN:

Saint Paul! It is not that.

FRIEND:

Then must it be
Your wealth. It is a heavy care to you,
Since you lack heir of your own blood.

EVERYMAN:

Nay, friend,
It is not that.

FRIEND:

No need for many words,
For you have trust in me: the will you've made
Is in safe hands, I'm sure, and leaves your wealth
All to your sweetheart.

EVERYMAN:

Nay, my best of friends!
But listen!

FRIEND:

Spare your tongue, dear Everyman,
For but few words will make me understand.

EVERYMAN:

A very different matter troubles me—
A graver thing indeed!

FRIEND:

Out with it now,
And swiftly! There is comfort in a friend.

EVERYMAN:

Ah, yes! You are my friend!

FRIEND:

Then why not speak?

Perchance your time drawn short.

EVERYMAN:

Alas! That were
Most sorrowful of all!

FRIEND:

Then, Everyman,
Speak promptly! Else, where would our friendship be?

EVERYMAN:

Ah! if I opened to you all my heart,
And your turned back made that appeal but vain,
Then tenfold were my sorrow and despair!

FRIEND:

That which I say, I do!

EVERYMAN:

I thank my Lord!
A far, far journey is ordained to me—
One long and difficult. Nor is that all;
For I before my Maker and my Judge
Must give account of all my wealth and life.
Wherefore come thou with me, my faithful friend,
As lately was your promise!

FRIEND:

God! what's this?
To make and break a promise—that were shame!
I blush to think of it.

EVERYMAN:

My friend!

FRIEND:

                              And yet,
Ere start of such a journey I should need
Much thought.

EVERYMAN:

         Much thought! You even promised me
That, dead or living, you would leave me not,
Although the road led straightway unto Hell!

FRIEND:

Aye! aye! such was my speech, with hand on heart;
But, truth to tell, this is no time for jests:
The occasion is most serious. Tell me, please;
The journey started, when would we return?

EVERYMAN:

Oh! never! never! till the Judgment Day!

FRIEND:

Then by God's death, if that the message was,
Here stick I! On that journey go I not!

EVERYMAN:

You will not go?

FRIEND:

                  I stay here! I am frank,
You know, and freely tell you all my thoughts:

On such a journey, for no living soul
Would I go forth!   Not for my father's sake,
God rest him!

EVERYMAN:

Christ! you promised otherwise!

FRIEND:

Well know I that I promised you to go,
And in good faith enough.   You ever were
Good company where women are concerned,
And were such sport in prospect, I should fail
You never, not so long as God should give
Us light by day and torches light by night.
And that's the truth!

(*Begins to go.*)

EVERYMAN:

Now does my need begin
Of you!   Now need I you in truth, good friend!

FRIEND:

Good friends or no, now take I never step
Henceforth with you!

EVERYMAN:

(*Taking him by the arm.*)
Nay, for God's mercy go
A little way!

FRIEND:

(*Tears himself away.*)

> Not I! I will not put
One foot before the other! No, not for
New festal robes! Had you more time to spare,
I would not let you wait alone: as 'tis,
I cannot tarry longer.
>> (*Over his shoulder.*)
>>> Heaven grant
A speedy trip, and at the journey's end
Your best well-being! Now must I make haste!

EVERYMAN:

> (*A step after him.*)
Whither away, my comrade? Would you leave
Me all alone?

FRIEND:

> What else? God keep your soul!

EVERYMAN:

Farewell, my friend! Heavy my heart for you!
Your health for aye! We shall not meet again!

FRIEND:

You too, farewell, O Everyman! Farewell
Unto the last! Your hand! Ah! parting hurts!
I know that now!
> (*Exit.*)

EVERYMAN:

> Alas! where shall I find
Help in this world? He was my friend so long
As I was merry. Now full plain he shows

His little sympathy. Ever I had
A sense of this, but would not let it sway
My mind, until this hour. Now falls the stroke.
'Tis always thus: so long as Fortune smiles
One shall have many friends. When Fortune turns
Her back, then watch them scatter! Ah! it seems
So dreadful! Fear and sorrow choke me! Christ!
(*Turns to Paramour.*)
Say you will come with me!

PARAMOUR:

What, go with you,
And youth still glad and singing in my heart,
And beauty still supreme on face and form,
And all life's joys to lure me? Did I go
I'd lose that pleasure-garden that you gave,
And all the thousand raptures of my days.
I'll dance with you on all the roads of bliss,
But on the Lonely Road I will not go!
So ask me not. Love's over now. Farewell!
(*Exit.*)

EVERYMAN:

Ah, God! Was ever misery like mine?
My very love forsakes me!
(*He becomes aware of his Cousins near by, and his face
lights up.*)
But there stand
My blood relations. Cousins dear, pray you,
Remain with me! You have come just in time.
There is no lovelier saying in the world
Than this: "Like draws to like." And this you prove

Today. With word and deed, in this dark hour,
Be you my boon companions!

FAT COUSIN:

Be you still
My cousin Everyman! And that is all
That needs be said. Be kinsman still of mine!

EVERYMAN:

You will not leave me?

FAT COUSIN:

Not a word! Who'd dream
To leave you in the lurch? That were a shame!

THIN COUSIN:

Whatever fares, deep sorrow or full joy,
We would share both with you.

FAT COUSIN:

Ah! True! Well said!
You see how faithfully we stand.

EVERYMAN:

Great thanks,
My kinsmen!

FAT COUSIN:

And because we are your kin—

EVERYMAN:

You saw the Messenger that came. He came

At the Great King's command.

FAT COUSIN:

Yes, yes, I know,
Cousin Everyman, but find the matter such
As lies beyond my mending.

EVERYMAN:

He commands
That I do make a journey.

FAT COUSIN:

So 'tis told.

EVERYMAN:

And from this journey—

FAT COUSIN:

Now, as said before,
"Like draws to like."

EVERYMAN:

And from this journey I,
Full well I know, shall nevermore return.

FAT COUSIN:

Never? Well, out of nothing, nothing comes.

EVERYMAN:

Dear cousin, hear you me?

FAT COUSIN:

You do not speak

To one who's deaf.

THIN COUSIN:

God's truth, that's true enough!

EVERYMAN:

I never shall return!

FAT COUSIN:

But did you hear
The Messenger aright?

EVERYMAN:

I?   Him?

FAT COUSIN:

The words
He said, and what he meant?   Did you catch all
Aright?

EVERYMAN:

Did I——?

FAT COUSIN:

Just so!   That's what I said.
A most unwelcome guest, eh, cousin?

THIN COUSIN:

Yes!
I mean——I pray to God——

FAT COUSIN:

You mean the same

As I.   Yes, as I said, God be with you,
Everyman! which is all that I can say!

EVERYMAN:

O cousins, stay and listen!

THIN COUSIN:

Have you, then,
Some other wish?   Announce it, cousin dear.

EVERYMAN:

There must I render my account, and find
A watchful Enemy whose single thought
Is my destruction.   Ah! with all your ears
Listen to me!

FAT COUSIN:

But tell me—what account?

EVERYMAN:

The account of all my earthly deeds, and how
My days were spent.   Yea! and what sins were mine,
By night and day, through all my guilty years.
And so, for Christ's sake, lift your hearts in prayer
And help me solve this thing!

THIN COUSIN:

What! do you mean
The road afar?   Nay, cousin Everyman!
I go not as your fellow-traveler
Thereon!   I rather in a gloomy cell
For all my years would live on prison fare.

EVERYMAN:

Oh! that I never had been born!   Oh! never
Shall I know happiness again if now
You twain desert me!

FAT COUSIN:

           Nay, man!   What is this?
Be of light heart!   Assert yourself!   Be firm!
I tell you, once and for all, you shall not drag
Me down with you!
          (Starts to go.)

EVERYMAN:

    (To Thin Cousin.)
          But Cousin, will not *you*
Set forth with me?

THIN COUSIN:

          Saint Clare!   I find I've got
Cramp in the toes—a grievous malady!
It came a-sudden.

FAT COUSIN:

(Remains standing and speaks over his shoulder.)
          Plague us not, for we
Cannot be tempted!   I've a sweetheart home
Who loves to travel: she might suit you should
You see her.   You are welcome to her.   She
Might go with you.

EVERYMAN:

          Declare now your intent!

Will you desert me in my misery?
There's this one thing that I must know: will you
Go with me or go not?

FAT COUSIN:

                    I stick at home.
But luck to you, dear Everyman! God speed,
Until we meet again!
          (*Cousins start to go.*)

EVERYMAN:

              O Saviour Christ!
Are all things at an end? They promised me
So much! And now they break their plighted word!

THIN COUSIN:

      (*Turns and approaches Everyman.*)
'Tis not our use, nor seems it fair and right,
To ask a person forth on such a trip.
Your body-servants should suffice: ask them.
Your kindred should be far too dear to you.

EVERYMAN:

My body-servants! That's a fine idea!
What use are they? I should have little help
From *them!*
         (*He looks around.*)
        Is there an end, now, to the feast?
Have all the revellers left the banquet-hall?
(*He goes up to the table. A few who are sitting and drinking notice him, jump up and flee. The table disappears.*)

Is there no other aid, and am I lost—
Alone in all the world?   Has God so planned?
Designs He so, that I be wholly stripped
And weak, as though already in my grave?
I, with the blood still warm in every vein?
I, whom my servants in all things obey?
I, with my wealth of houses and of gold?
Up! Sound the fire-alarm!   Ye lazy scamps,
Loaf not about the house!   Come quickly!   Come!
        (*Steward hastens out with several servants.*)
I must essay a journey speedily—
On foot at that: no carriage. All must go—
These servants. All my money-coffers, too,
They must be borne. 'Twill be like going forth
To war. I'll be in need of all my wealth.

STEWARD:

The heavy money-coffers?

EVERYMAN:

                    Yes! Make haste
With no more talk!
        (*Servants bring chest out carefully.*)
                    I've called you for a trip,
And see you show obedience! The way
Is strange and very far, and needs thereon
Only the most trustworthy folk. This is
A secret, and I hope you keep it one.

SERVANT:

Painfully heavy is this chest!

STEWARD:

Obey
The master's will!

EVERYMAN:

Now set we forth, most still
And secretly.
(Death comes from the distance.)

FIRST SERVANT:

Look! look! A devil! Look!
He signs to us to halt!

STEWARD:

Nay! it is Death,
The dreadful one! In all his power he comes.
(Servants leave chest standing and run. Steward runs too.)

DEATH:

O fool! Soon comes your hour, and still you stand
All unprepared! You know not how to find
The right companionship. Soon will you doubt,
And curse yourself!
(Vanishes.)

EVERYMAN:

O God! how dread I death!
Cold is my brow with sweat of my despair!
Say, can the soul be murdered in the flesh?
What comes on me swiftly? I have found
Some comfort ever in my darkest hours,
And ne'er been wholly left alone, a poor

And pitiable fool!   Ever I had
A rock on which to hold, and clung thereto
With all my strength.   Are all my powers gone,
My mind deranged already, that I fail
To know me who I am?—rich Everyman,
Who thought to live forever!   Everyman!
This is my hand and this my garment.   There
My treasure stands, the gold that was my strength
And ever swiftly won me my desire.
Surely before mine eyes I see my wealth:
Could I remain by it, no fear were mine,
No grim anxiety; but now, alas!
Sudden I realize I must go forth!
The messenger was here, the summons cried,
And now must I go hence!
                    (*Throws himself on the chest.*)
                                    Not without you!
You must go forth with me!   Oh! not for aught
Would I leave *you* behind!   You must go hence
With me unto another House!   So come!
Come quickly with me out of this!
        (*Chest springs open.   MAMMON rises from it.*)

MAMMON:

                                    Ho—ho!
What ails you, Everyman?   You seem to be
In mighty haste, and meanwhile white as chalk!

EVERYMAN:

Who, then, are you?

MAMMON:

You know me not, and yet
Would drag me with you? Lo! of all your wealth
Am I the keeper—guard of all you own
On earth!

EVERYMAN:

Your countenance does please me not,
Nor gives me bravery. Yet all the same
Must you go with me.

MAMMON:

Where's the sense in that?
What needs be done, that can we here perform.
Behold my might! Say what oppresses you:
Then can I be of aid.

EVERYMAN:

'Tis otherwise,
This time: I have been summoned.

MAMMON:

Yes—and by?—

EVERYMAN:

(*With downcast eyes.*)
There came for me a Messenger.

MAMMON:

And so
For that you must go hence? A messenger!
And come to summon you! A sudden thing!
I never heard the like before!

EVERYMAN:

And you
Go also: thus I order!

MAMMON:

Not a step!
I've too much comfort here.

EVERYMAN:

But you are mine!
My all! My property!

MAMMON:

I yours? Ha-ha!
Don't make me laugh!

EVERYMAN:

You would rebel? Vile thing!
Accursed one!

MAMMON:

(Pushing him aside.)
Be not too sure of me:
I care not for your wrath! The thing's reversed:
I am the giant now, and you the dwarf!
You are the servant now, my little man!
Dreamed you 'twas ever otherwise? That were
But self-deception and a fool's idea.

EVERYMAN:

I had you at my orders.

MAMMON:

             And I reigned
Within your soul.

EVERYMAN:

         You were, in house and street,
My servant.

MAMMON:

         At the end of a held string
I let you dance.

EVERYMAN:

          You were my body-servant
And slave.

MAMMON:

       No! you were my brave jumping-jack.

EVERYMAN:

But I alone dared touch you.

MAMMON:

              I alone
Could lead you by the nose. Poor knave! Raw fool!
Oh! fool of fools? Why look you, Everyman:
I stay behind on earth, and where go you?
The strength I placed in you, the giant power,
What have you made of it?——a spectacle,
A glittering show, a fashioned pompousness,
A lustful, cursed fury! He was but
A bladder blown by me, and that he soared
And still can soar, is due alone to me.

This is what gave him courage to exist.

(*Lifts a handful of money from chest, and lets it fall back
again.*)

Back whence it came it falls: there also ends
Your happiness! Soon too your senses five
Shall wither, till you know me not again.
I was but lent you for this earthly day,
And go not on your journey. I? Depart?
Nay, I remain! You shall go forth, alone,
In want and fell despair. In vain for you
The stretching out of hands! In vain for you
To wail or gnash your teeth! You shall go forth
Naked and bare as when you reached this world!

(*Bows down. .Chest shuts. Everyman speechless. A
long pause. GOOD DEEDS becomes visible, like a
sick person stretched on a wretched pallet. She raises
herself a little and calls in a feeble voice.*)

GOOD DEEDS:

Everyman!

(*He pays no attention.*)
Do you not hear me, Everyman?

EVERYMAN:

(*To himself.*)

It is as though one called. The voice is weak,
Yet very clear. Now, God forbid it be
My mother! She is feeble, old and frail:
May she be spared this sight! For pity's sake
May it not be my mother!

GOOD DEEDS:

Everyman!

EVERYMAN:

Oh! be it who it may, I have no time
For worldly matters and annoyances.

GOOD DEEDS:

Do you not hear me, Everyman?

EVERYMAN:

It is

Some ill and weakly woman.   What care I?
At such a time she must fend for herself.

GOOD DEEDS:

To you, O Everyman! do I belong.
Behold me lying here because of you!

EVERYMAN:

How can that be?

GOOD DEEDS:

(Half raises herself.)
I am the deeds you did.

Behold me!

EVERYMAN:

Mock me not, for at this hour
I am a dying man!

GOOD DEEDS:

Draw near to me

This little way.

(Sinks back.)

EVERYMAN:

Unwilling gaze I *now*
Upon my mortal deeds: they are no sight
For me.

GOOD DEEDS:

Most weak am I, and must lie here:
Were it but possible, I'd run to you.

EVERYMAN:

I want no other person's cares. I have
Enough of fear and misery for myself.

GOOD DEEDS:

Yet need you me. The way is fearsome far,
And you have no companion.

EVERYMAN:

I must go
That way alone.

GOOD DEEDS:

Nay! I will go with you,
For I am yours.

(Everyman looks toward her.)

GOOD DEEDS:

It is great grief to me,
A heavy burden on my soul, that you
Have given me no thought, since, but for you,

I could move swiftly, and in all events
Be at your side.

EVERYMAN:

(*Goes to her.*)
Good Deeds, most ill it fares
With me this hour. Oh! for some good advice!
For any aid!

GOOD DEEDS:

(*Tries hard to raise herself on her crutches.*)
I have heard, Everyman,
That you before your Saviour have been called
And the tremendous Judgment. Go not forth
Alone, I say, unless you would be lost!

EVERYMAN:

Will you go with me?

GOOD DEEDS:

Will I go with you?
You ask me that, O Everyman?

EVERYMAN:

(*Gazing into her eyes.*)
You look
At me so longingly! In all my life
Methinks, no man nor woman—lover, friend—
Gazed on me with such eyes.

GOOD DEEDS:

Oh! Everyman!
That you at this late hour should turn unto

Mine eyes and mouth!

EVERYMAN:

You have a careworn face,
And pale, but rich in loveliness to me.
The more I look on you, so much the more
My heart is moved.   Now tender are my thoughts,
Yet so confused I do not know myself.
It is as though your eyes so gleamed that they
Could lighten mine.   Great blessing and great peace
Would come to a poor man.   But surely I
Have failed, and now it all is but a dream!

GOOD DEEDS:

Had you but known I'm not unbeautiful,
And, faithful at my side, remained away
From evil and the world—draw near, my voice
Is low—had you gone out among the poor,
Full brotherly, in reverence, and had you
Begun to cherish holy grief and pain,
Your heart had grown, and I, so feeble now,
I should have been transfigured in your sight.
This would have been to you a heavenly Cup,
A Chalice with God's mercy brimming o'er,
And set in invitation to your lips!

EVERYMAN:

Oh! and I might have never seen your face,
So blind was I!   What creatures of the dark
Are we, alas! when such can be our doom!

GOOD DEEDS:

I was a chalice set before your sight—

A chalice filled by Heaven to the brim.
There was no taint of earthliness therein,
And therefore seemed I little in your eyes.

EVERYMAN:

Oh! I could tear them out! I would not be
So fearful of the darkness then, for they
Have led me on to bitterness of woe,
Falsely, and all life long.

GOOD DEEDS:

                        Alas! your lips
Must now be parched forevermore! Your thirst
Desired the world for drink: now is the cup
Refused.

EVERYMAN:

                  Therefore do I already feel
Within these veins a thirst more terrible.
My senses rave! This is my life's reward!

GOOD DEEDS:

So bitter is repentance! So it burns!
These are the sufferings you should have known.
Could now your heart experience them, what bliss
It were for us!

EVERYMAN:

(*Prostrates himself.*)

                  Let me be ground to dust
From head to heel, if in this mortal frame
One fibre lives that cries not wild with woe

And deep repentance! To re-live my days!
But no! Another chance! It cannot be!
Nay, though I fear and shriek, I shall not live
A second life! Now my torn bosom knows,
Unknown till now, the meaning of those words,
"Lie down to die! The knell has struck! All ends."

GOOD DEEDS:
(*On her knees.*)
Shall this repentance flaming and immense
Not free me from the ground? For I would rise
Unto my feet, and stand by him this hour!
(*Falls to ground.*)
Oh! I am ill and feeble!

EVERYMAN:
O'er our deeds
Merciless justice hangs! Ah! leave me not
To face my Judge alone! Not that! Not that!
Surely I should be lost! Oh! help you me
To render my account to Him the Lord
Of life and death, King of Eternity!
Else am I lost forever!

GOOD DEEDS:
Everyman!

EVERYMAN:

Leave me not without counsel!

GOOD DEEDS:
Know you then
I have a sister, gentle but austere,

A guide from guilt to mercy, Faith her name.
Let us appeal to her: could she be moved
By humble prayer, she might abide with you,
And with you go before the throne of God.

EVERYMAN:

Hasten! Time flies! For God's sake summon her!

GOOD DEEDS:

It may be she will turn from you, and then
You must go to the grave uncomforted.
Yet would she give you of her help, could you
Talk with her rightly.

EVERYMAN:

                    If one had no tongue,
Fear and necessity would give him one.
                    (FAITH enters.)

GOOD DEEDS:

Needless were it to talk so loud. I feel
My sister comes. Dear sister, deep distress
Is on this mortal: will you stay with him
At death? For all my strength goes out of me.
Feeble, I cannot aid him in his need.
                    (Falls back.)

FAITH:

                    (To Everyman.)
For all your life have you held me in scorn,
Scorning God's word as well. Now, at death's hour,
Is there a different tenor to your speech?

EVERYMAN:

I believe!   I believe!

FAITH:

           The speech is poor!

EVERYMAN:

O God! have mercy! deeply I believe
In the twelve articles and all that they
Embrace! Established are they unto me,
And holy!

FAITH:

      'Tis the poorer part of faith:
Build not too much on such a penitence.
Have you so poor contrition?

EVERYMAN:

                I believe

In God's long sufferance, if one repent
In time. But I am sunk so deep in sin
His mercy cannot reach me.

FAITH:

      (Takes a step nearer him.)
               Are you, then,
So deeply drowned in lust, so steeped in sin,
That now your lips are barren of the word
Which might forever save your forfeit soul?
          (Kneels before him.)

EVERYMAN:

I believe!

FAITH:

Do you believe in Jesus Christ,
Come to us from the Father? Like ourselves
A mortal man, of mortal woman born,
Who for your sake poured out His precious blood
And has arisen from the dead, that you
With God His Father might be reconciled!

EVERYMAN:

Yea! I believe! All this He did for us,
He calmed His Father's wrath, and on the Cross
Died in His blamelessness, to bring mankind
Salvation everlasting. Yet I know
The good alone shall take avail of this,
Whose righteousness and piety shall gain
For them the life eternal. But behold
My deeds! Alas! the mountain of my sins
Crushes me down! God cannot pardon me,
Being the All-High Judge!

FAITH:

And are you such
A doubting Christian? Know you not the depth
Of God's great mercy?

EVERYMAN:

Surely, terribly,
God punishes!

FAITH:

He pardons without measure!

EVERYMAN:

Pharaoh He slew! On Sodom and Gomorrah
Rained He His fire!

FAITH:

And gave His only Son
To this sad world. From Heaven He sent Him forth
That He be born a man, and so no man
Be lost—that one and all, e'en to the last
Might find eternal life. "Lo! I am come,"
He said, "to save the sinner, and not him
Who needeth no repentance!" So He spake .
Who cannot lie. If you believe ere death
Then is your sin forgiven, and God's wrath
Is stilled.

EVERYMAN:

Your words are gentle. Oh! I feel
As I were born anew! So long as I
Draw breath on earth, so long do I believe
That through the Christ our Lord I may be saved!

FAITH:

Because you do believe, go hence and wash
Your soul from sin!

EVERYMAN:

Where is there such a Spring
Oh holy water? Oh! to reach it soon!
(A Monk becomes visible above.)

FAITH:

A holy man awaits you, by whose help
Your soul shall yet be purified. Return,

This done, clad all in white, and I will take
Your hand and go with you—I, you, good deeds!
So shall you gain in strength.

EVERYMAN:

(On his knees.)
                                    Eternal God!
Oh! Beatific Vision!   Road of Truth,
And heavenly Light!   Here at my final hour
I cry to Thee, and wailing fills this mouth!
O Savior dear, pray my Creator now
That He be merciful unto the end,
When the dark Enemy draws near from Hell
And Death's appalling clutch is at my throat!
Pray that He take my soul above, that I
Through thy sweet intercession may approach,
O Christ, thy seat at His right hand, and go
With Him in glory!   Let this be my pray'r,
For thou upon the Cross hast saved our souls!
*(He lies in prayer upon his face.   Organ sounds louder; at
    the same time, in the darkness, Everyman's Mother
    crosses over, as to early Mass, her servant carrying a
    torch.   She pauses.)*

SERVANT:

Madame, why stand you still, and at this hour?
What ails you?   Are you ill?   Were it not best
That you return unto your home and bed
Than hasten to this early Mass?

EVERYMAN'S MOTHER:

                                    Are we

So late? Is Mass beginning now? I hear
Marvellous ringing, as though angels sang.

SERVANT:

In no wise are we late, nor do I hear
Sounds loud or low.

EVERYMAN'S MOTHER:

                                I hear, and in my heart
I know they are the angelic songs that rise
About God's throne! It is for my dear son!
At this good hour his soul is healed, and he
Is reconciled unto the Lord our God.
Now joyously and willingly I die.
My prayer is heard. I know that I shall stand
Before my God, before my Savior's throne,
And find my dear son there. Now lettest Thou
Thy servant journey forth in peace! Amen!

SERVANT:

Madame, will not you come? Time flies. 'Tis dark!
(*They pass on.*)

FAITH:

May God be with you, Everyman! And as
I call you forth this hour and bid you go
Before your Saviour, so be your account
Made errorless, and free from earthly guilt.

GOOD DEEDS:

Alas! I fain would rise but am too weak!
(*Enter DEBTOR and WORKMAN.*)

DEBTOR:

Now suffer that we help you rise.

WORKMAN:

Our limbs
Are strong, yours feeble.

GOOD DEEDS:

Who am I that you
Should aid me now?   Am I not strange to you?
Have I been kind to you that you to me
Should proffer kindness?   It is in my heart
That you have had but wrongs from Everyman.

DEBTOR:

Hard was his hand on me, but now a Hand
More terrible is on him: I forgive,
For that is first among a Christian's needs.

WORKMAN:

We toilers are a poor and simple folk,
Nor hoard our wrongs, but cheerfully forgive.
(*Good Deeds throws her crutches away and approaches
him.*)

FAITH:

O Everyman, prepare yourself for joy!
For now in truth are your good deeds made straight,
And free from all the burden of your sin!

GOOD DEEDS:

See!   It is I your friend, O Everyman!

I bless you, who have freed me from my pain,
And will go with you, wheresoe'er it be.

EVERYMAN:

Ah! dear Good Deeds!   I weep for very joy
To hear your voice!

FAITH:

                    Now must you sorrow not,
Nor longer weep.   Nay! now indeed rejoice,
And show a happy spirit.   From His throne
God sees you healed.

EVERYMAN:

                    I seek no more delay
Nor lingering.   My friends, we shall go forth
Together, for I shall not part from you.
(*He goes up and follows after monk. Faith and Good
Deeds persist in praying.*)

DEVIL:

            (*Comes bounding in.*)
Hold, Everyman!   Stop, Everyman!   Halt, halt!
Come hither, comrade!   Here I stand, who came
To fetch you.   I am here.   Ho, Everyman!
He's gone within!   He must be very deaf,
And in both ears!.   Why enters he that house?
Ye others, hale him forth, and I meanwhile
Will wait outside.   Catch him and bring him here!
It may be he will keep me waiting long.
Let him!   I fear not that: he's in my clutch,
Body and soul, as never man before.

FAITH:

Hold!

DEVIL:

(*Does not hear.*)
I must pass!

FAITH:

Not here the way!

DEVIL:

It is,

For I have business there.

FAITH:

Here for your kind

There is no way.

DEVIL:

A woman, quarrelsome!

I can evade her.

FAITH:

(*Gets in his way again.*)
Here's no way for you!

DEVIL:

On business must I stand beside yon door,
So that, when he I seek comes forth, I then
Can take him with me on a certain way.

FAITH:

I will not argue with you.

DEVIL:

Nor will I
With you.   But I will pass.

GOOD DEEDS:

Here is no way
For you.

DEVIL:

(*Closes up his ears.*)
Noise!   Noise!   A pest!

GOOD DEEDS:

(*Gets in his way.*)
No way!

DEVIL:

No way?
No way?   Is there no way?   No ground on which
My feet may stand?   No place to leap?   Then I
Forthwith will make a way!
(*Tries to go through by force.*)

FAITH:

(*Stepping forward.*)
Would you, then, use
Your very fists?   Disturb our holy pray'rs?
Behold who comes to aid us!
(*Angel comes from above.*)

DEVIL:

Ha-ha-ha!
So all our gentle friends are in the game!
They whose sole task it is to lounge and gape,

From morn till nightfall, while their betters go
About their duty with all urgency,—
With eagerness and great expense of strength!
(*Good Deeds and Faith do not look at him, but pray with
folded hands.*)
Hell's bottom! Is there any doubt in this?
Shall there be argument? Incredible!
Lives there on earth a soul that would deny,
Here to my face, this man is lost to me?
This mighty glutton! This great tank of wine!
This woman-hunter and adulterer!
This tempter, loose in word and deed, with less
Belief than a black heathen has, and more
Forgetful of his God than are the brutes
Of field and stye! This waster of the goods
Of widows and of orphans! This oppressor!
This hater!
(Springs up.)
Where are words to picture him?
They fail me, such a sinful beast is he!
Yet they refuse him to me, when that I
Would grasp him, twist his neck, and yell to him:
"Abase thee, mortal clay, and die!" Yea! thus
Cold-bloodedly I'd wait for him, and seize
His soul for Hell! And shall you then not fear
My wrath, my gnashing jaws, my doubled fist?
Shall you not see that justice and the right
Stand armed at my side?

FAITH:
At your side
None stands. You have already lost the game,
And God ere now has balanced in His scales

The penitence and debt of Everyman,
To find what should eternally be paid.

DEVIL:

How shall that be? Shall then an hour outweigh
The habits of a life? Shall one wax fat,
And, calmly and deliberately, base
His life on sin, and, day and night, upbuild
The ramparts of his guilt, then, at the last,
Find the substantial and considered pile
A thing a single blow can overwhelm?

FAITH:

Yea! thus Repentance works! She has a strength,
A fire to recreate the ruined soul
From sin's own dust and ashes!

DEVIL:

                              Woman's tricks
And chatter! Wash my fur and wet it not!
Wish-washy twaddle! I could spit with hate!
Proofs! Proofs! Give proofs! Show me one word or deed
To put him in the right before a judge!

FAITH:

Before that Judge to Whom he goes today,
Your right would go for nothing. It is based
On earthly fraud and pretense, and by Time
Has limitation, tangled in Time's mesh....
Where ring those bells?
(One hears from within the death-bells. .Good Deeds and
            Faith fall to their knees.)

GOOD DEEDS:

Eternity begins!

DEVIL:

(*Closing his ears.*)

Enough! I quit! O leave him! I go home!
Pamper your pet! I shudder with disgust!
(*Good Deeds and Faith have raised themselves.*)
A happy case, as clear as day, and yet
A hair is in the soup, and all's a waste!
Fearless and merry step I to the front
And call me heritor of this damn'd soul,
To hear: "No thoroughfare! No thoroughfare!"
Prison and lash to you, you long-robed things!
The very heathen had allowed my claim—
It would have been mere justice! Now they shout:
"No thoroughfare!"—these women! Hell is hot,
And here he comes white-robed, arch hypocrite!
And whining for his sins! The world is bad,
Stupid and mean! Here might alone is right!
The world is rank injustice, and full oft
Would injure us sincere and clever folk! (*Exit
Everyman comes from above, in long white robe,
a pilgrim's staff in his hand, and his face
deathly white, but transfigured. Approaches the two.*)

GOOD DEEDS:

See I not Everyman draw near? 'Tis he!
He has made peace with God, and strengthened us
For a sure flight to Heaven.

LaVergne, TN USA
14 December 2009
166883LV00011B/13/P